# Welcome!

*from our fierce founder*

Welcome to issue 18 of *Fierce Truths Magazine*! With this issue I feel a call to deepen into the earth a little more than I have allowed myself to before. Perfect timing for us all really, to help us navigate these special (and chaotic) times.

That is why this month, I am excited to introduce you to Orly Faya, an artist with a special mission here on earth, to paint us into the earth. Using her work to awaken us to a foundational truth, that we come from the earth, and we are one with the earth. A connection we can't live without. Her interview has certainly validated my own calling, and what I am (and not) doing about that. Which I hope it does for you too.

We are all in this together remember.

Of course, our other articles are just as insightful and important to your growth and a spiritual beingness. We look at what it means to be spiritually mature, because it ain't all love and light, and how being selfless can lead to being less ourselves.

We also interview Root and Nourish authors Abbey and Jennifer. and talk food as medicine and the importance of living that in our life.

Our intent with every issue of *Fierce Truths Magazine* is to inspire, transform and spiritually educate you. Giving you the tools you need to activate that best version of yourself. So, I **Hope that one of our articles will remind you of how extraordinary you are, and how incredible your life can be.**

*With fierce love,*

**KIM BLEEZE**
Founder & Vision Holder
*FIERCE TRUTHS MAGAZINE*

Follow us on social media
@fiercetruthsmagazine

# CONTENTS

## Monthly Musing

Monthly advice with our fierce team of experts! **43**

# OUR TEAM

## Editorial

**Kim Bleeze**
Editor-in-chief | Creative Director | Lay-out Design

**Scott Grasso**
Editor

**Kylie Clarke**
Proof-reader

**Elizabeth Vigar**
In-house writer

**Andrew Karabatos**
Cover Designer | Layout Consultant

## Our Fierce Experts

**Lisa Westgate**
Mind Your Mental Wellness

**Scott Grasso**
Radical Thinking

**Karina Barca**
Empowered Healing

**Lindie Gunston**
Spirit & Soul

**Jo Lastro**
Fierce Fitness

**Michelle Luehman**
SpiritWise

## Guest Contributors

**Kinga Elizabeth Staszalek**
Spiritual Maturity

**John Bride**
The Miracle of Metatron

**Carrie Myers**
SelfLess

**Orly Faya**
Featured Interview - Painted Earth

**Abbey Rodriguez and Jennifer Kurdyla**
Interview with Root & Nourish authors

## Staff

**Marissa Colosimo**
Social Media Engagement

## Contact

**Management & Advertising**
fierce@fiercetruthsmagazine.com

**Support & Inquiries**
ask@fiercetruthsmagazine.com

Find yourself...
by getting lost

# Spiritual Maturity

## SPIRITUALITY AS A MUST TO FREEDOM AND FULFILMENT

By Kinga Elizabeth Staszalek

**The starting point of spirituality is understanding ourselves and the meaning of our existence.**

Spirituality is the ability to answer the question: Who are you? Where did you come from? Where are you going? How can you achieve your life goals? How can you be free and fulfilled?

Spirituality allows you to consciously lead your own life. Thanks to spirituality, you are able to take a conscious and responsible attitude towards yourselves, other people and the whole world.

# MATERIAL AND SPIRITUAL NEEDS

We live in times where the majority of people's longing for spiritual growth disappears or it does not appear at all. We want to be materially rich rather than spiritually rich.

Unfortunately, if we are immature and spiritually limited, we are unable to make reasonable use of material prosperity even if we achieved such prosperity or success. Despite the success, we often don't experience peace or abundance. We need to seek more than material or physical well-being.

# FALSE SPIRITUALITY

Even when we learn about spirituality, we often misunderstand it as something that is not really spirituality. For example, emotional state, artistic sensitivity, deep feelings, admiration for nature or exercises for breathing, stillness - all these are not spirituality. These types of skills and exercises while important and positive, do not guarantee that you will understand yourselves and the meaning of your existence.

# OUR PSYCHE AND LIMITATIONS

We also try to understand spirituality from the psychological point of view, but it doesn't help us with a deep sense of belonging or purposeful living. Instead, we focus on subjective beliefs or emotional experiences. We need to understand that our psyche is not the source of our being, nor the source of the truth about ourselves.

This sphere is the intellectual and emotional reaction of our own current life situation as well as past experiences. We can only understand our thoughts and beliefs about ourselves on the basis of the opinions we form while experiencing life, yet we still cannot understand ourselves fully.

# OUR MIND AND PROJECTIONS

The human mind is not the source of knowledge about nature and humanity. The mind can discover this secret, learn new knowledge but cannot by its own power, invent or establish it. Our mind does not seek the truth about who we truly are, but subjective opinions that are convenient, to live life safely and justify the reality we live in. When we rely on the mind as the highest authority to follow, we deceive ourselves and miss the whole point of discovering what is beyond our mind. In this way, we deprive ourselves of the chance to understand ourselves and achieve true growth, evolution and alignment.

# EMOTIONAL ILLUSION

It is most challenging for humans to cultivate a mature attitude towards our own emotional experiences. If we are unable to take responsibility for our emotional state, we are also unable to communicate with another person without a projection caused by our painful previous experiences. When negative memories take over our behaviours and actions, it often leads to avoiding contact with painful emotions. We then try to understand our emotional state through the mind or logic. Sometimes we even put ourselves above the emotions and we delude ourselves that we don't feel emotions. Spiritual maturity means that all emotions inform us about the situation we are in, but do not rule our decisions or actions taken. We can feel all emotions, overcome challenges, physical or emotional pain and we achieve what we dream the most in life. Nowadays we tend to escape into the world of the illusion that spirituality is living in a state of constant bliss, peace and only experiencing positive feelings or even feeling nothing.

Nothing could be more wrong, because spirituality is the freedom to feel, to be fully yourself, to express yourself. We are free beings to experience everything in life as human and spiritual beings at the same time.

We can distinguish between our own limiting beliefs, make decisions based on love, courage, truth and responsibility, not based on painful experiences or the limitations of the mind.

# SPIRITUALITY AND MATURITY

Spiritual maturity means you not only understand your own mystery, complexity in a true accepting and profound way, but also have a chance to experience yourself and lead yourself through core values and your own goals. You also create real committed connections with people based on love, authenticity and growth. Only as a spiritually mature person you can think, feel, love, work, be fulfilled and feel free in life.

# KNOWLEDGE VERSUS WISDOM

With all the knowledge that is available to us, we understand the world around us better and better, but unfortunately, we understand ourselves less and less. As a consequence, we rely on the information, the exchange of knowledge about the world and a fiction about the meaning of our existence. This often leads to our crisis, a feeling of being unfulfilled, loneliness, emptiness and suffering.

Therefore, concern for the spiritual maturity should be the foundation of our growth so that we understand ourselves at the deepest level. We will be able to establish real relationships with ourselves, with other people and with the whole universe. Then we will feel the freedom to be ourselves, experience life to fullest without any emotional or mental restraints, then in the spiritual and truest way, we will derive knowledge from the essence of our existence.

Kinga Elizabeth Staszalek is a love and relationship coach expert, energy healer and founder of Lapis Evolution. Inspired by her own personal development and spiritually awakening journey, Kinga helps people to heal from past, growth spiritually with mature wisdom, manifest real love, ideal partners and create life of their dreams.

Visit her website at *lapisevolution.com*

JUST
bre

athe

# FOOD AS MEDICINE

## REBALANCE YOUR
## EMOTIONAL, PHYSCIAL & SPIRITUAL HEALTH

AN INTERVIEW WITH
# ABBEY RODRIGUEZ AND JENNIFER KURDYLA
## AUTHORS OF *ROOT & NOURISH*

*Written by Elizabeth Vigar*
*Fierce Truths Magazine*

Through their spiritual journeys, Abbey Rodriguez's and Jennifer Kurdyla's paths crossed, and they couldn't ignore what the Universe was telling them: that they had to embark on a creative project together.

After realising that they both had many shared expertise, they decided to combine their knowledge and write a book. That project became Root & Nourish, a book that embraces a holistic approach to feminine health, encompassing spirituality, nutrition, sleep, movement, and connection with ourselves and the planet. *Root & Nourish* is a spiritual guide as much as it is a very literal nutrition guide.

Abbey Rodriguez is a blogger, mother, wife, recipe developer, food stylist, and photographer. In 2018 she was diagnosed with Celiac disease and a hypothyroidism autoimmune disease. As difficult as this diagnosis was, Abbey remained optimistic about the future, and through the changes she made to her diet, she realised that food is powerful medicine. Her recipes are gluten-free and primarily plant-based.

*"(The book) is holistic in the sense that there is something for everybody in there, and one aspect informs the other. It's not just a reductionist way of thinking. It's a very fluid intersecting web of all of these concepts and how they inform one another and how they need to coexist collectively together to allow harmony into our lives."*

Jennifer Kurdyla is an Ayurvedic health counsellor, yoga teacher, writer, and she has been a vegan since 2008. She has always been exploring ways to expand and enjoy her vegan lifestyle, and, as an editor for vegan cookbooks, she has spent years working on various vegan blogs and adapting them to print. Her passion is creating healthy foods that are accessible to more people.

*"For me being plant-based and being vegan opened my eyes to a relationship with food that is beyond just me. I felt much more connected to nature and the process of self-nourishment."*

Both women have grown their understanding of women's health, and their book focuses on digestion, mental health, and hormonal health. Jennifer says they saw this trend in spiritual femininity being lost or adulterated in our lives. Women are losing their ability to slow down, receive, and be deeply grounded and aligned with nature in its rhythmic cycles. These fundamental and straightforward rhythms like eating and listening to our intuition are drowned out by society, which, Jennifer says, has become more exacerbated and evident during the pandemic. Both women believe that they couldn't have created this book at a more appropriate and necessary time. *"Lessons about intuitive eating are coming back into the kitchen,"* says Jennifer.

Many people are suffering from impaired digestion without knowing it. Root & Nourish talks about the imbalances we experience, both individually and collectively, that stem from a lack of connection with our food. The book intends to make sure that the herbs and spices that we take as medicine are properly used by our bodies. Plant medicine needn't be a complicated concept; rather, it can be as simple as introducing more whole foods into your diet and understanding that they are plant medicines in and of themselves. Learning how to listen intuitively to what your body needs is the key.

*"The lack of knowledge that we have about nutrition and what is nutrient-dense and what is not is quite surprising. We take our food for granted, and I think the spiritual aspect of connecting to the plants, connecting to the Earth, connecting to your food, and having a sense of stewardship over the Earth encourages a greater reverence and respect,"* says Abbey.

**Root & Nourish also comes from an environmental perspective about food, leading us towards becoming more responsible for healing the planet.**

The recipes in Root & Nourish encourage us to reconnect to our food sources to preserve the Earth. A part of reconnecting with our Divine Feminine is to embrace a more expansive view of the world and practice being more mindful of the resources we have at hand and not just blindly using them. "There is an idea of cyclicality and rhythm that is inherent to the idea of the Divine Feminine that I think has been lost in our society," says Jennifer. Embracing the Divine Feminine is part of a spiritual journey where we intentionally connect with the herbs we put into our bodies and reclaim our feminine power.

"We, as women, definitely have this opportunity to lead and take care of the planet and make the changes we need to save Earth. This is a real issue we are dealing with, and those who read this book can hopefully feel that and feel empowerment within the pages and the message we are sharing," says Abbey.

Abbey and Jennifer hope that their readers will use Root & Nourish as a guide to becoming more connected to their emotional, physical, and spiritual health by listening to and respecting their bodies. Ultimately, empowering people to get into the kitchen, experiment, play, be inspired, and see food as medicine. They envision a safe place where people have access to support from other like-minded people where we all can bring Root & Nourish to life and share in rituals together.

*"Even if we have helped influence one person's life by helping them understand that the imbalances that they're feeling are due to a lack of connection to themselves, to their divine feminine, to the earth, to their food...then we have done our job."*

# AMBASSADOR PROGRAM

Do you have
what it takes?

JOIN US

Receive exclusive

Perks!

...and the opportunity to earn

fiercetruthsmagazine.com/ambassadorprogram

# Orly Faya

# PAINTED EARTH

Interview by Kim Bleeze

The earth has had a part to play in our lives from the moment we are born. and artist Orly Faya plays a very important role is awakening people to what she believes is our most foundational truth.

That Earth is our mother, and while our spirit may come from elsewhere, our physical being comes from the earth, a connection we can't live without. So by opening ourselves to the earth, we offer the opportunity to live a beautiful harmony of heaven of Earth.

A lifetime artist, philosopher and teacher, Orly's passion has flowed into her life in a way that is truly unique to her, using her artistic talent to paint her subjects into their background. Giving them the opportunity to not only meet themselves in such a profound way, but to be truly seen. Inspiring self-growth, transformation, deeper healing and change.

*"They want to honor something bigger than their personality and their identity. To dissolve into the Earth and to tap into something greater than any description of self could ever master."*

Although Orly is now based in Sydney Australia, her work and travel has taken her all around the world, influencing her artistic style, beliefs and mission here on earth.

Simply put, she loves to love all things beautiful and has allowed that to inspire the variety of her life's work.

We hope you feel as inspired by her interview as we do.

15 Fierce Truths Magazine

**Kim: In your own words, who is Orly Faya and what is she about?**

Orly: I was dubbed, 'The Little Philosopher' at my primary school graduation and have continued to philosophize since. I am an explorer, adventurer, in that I live in constant enquiry about what it means to be a human being and how to live in a way that serves the greater spirit of our collective consciousness.

Today, I teach people how to access the infinite vortex of possibility so they can learn how to become powerful creators of their dreams and live a life of fulfilment. I support people in living life fully, compassionately and graciously, using breath as a guiding force. Together, we can awaken to our potential as humans on earth.

Eighteen years of solo world travel has given me deep empathy for the diversity of humanity and an appreciation of the various experiences that make up the tapestry of our world. My passion for all things beautiful has led to my work in the arts, from the digital realms to painting bodies.

My love of nature has led to my environmental activism, in collaboration with World Wild Fund, Planet Ark, The Biosphere Foundation, Bob Brown Foundation and others. My commitment to integrity has taught me to honor my word and tap into the authenticity of the moment to find answers.

My happiest moments have been the simplest; living in a hut with only the basics, having less rather than more, being with people I love, surrounded by nature - this is home.

Journeying with plant medicine and Indigenous wisdoms has shown me what is truly important in life - and what is not.

I have flitted between green grasses, only to discover that the grass really is only greener from a distance. A big part of developing our spiritual muscle is to be at peace with where we are and with what is. No matter where we go, we find ourselves. Inner transformation leads to infinite freedom.

## I do not fit into a category and I celebrate this by offering my unique perspective and wisdom to all who wish to break out of the stories that dictate what is possible in their lives.

**Kim: Orly, let's talk about your work painting people into their background because it's fascinating.**

Orly: It's quite a story, but basically I was in the entertainment - circus kind of area and I was also painting faces. Then I saw a friend fully body painted and she looked incredible. I wrote a comment on the post and the woman who painted her was so encouraging and told me to give it a try, so I did.

My journey with body painting started a year prior to painting people into the world. It wasn't a mimicism, it wasn't a camouflage and it was a huge success from the start. I then won a competition and I was just inundated with people who wanted to be painted. I've come from an artistry background and have painted since I was a little girl, so I've been in love with it from the get-go.

I then went through a big breakup and on the week of the breakup, I was hired by an agency to paint a woman

# "Life on earth is the greatest miracle."

Orly Faya

Image Credits: Orly Faya's Professional Collection

into a backdrop of Sea Turtles for a World Wildlife campaign. I had never done anything like that before, but I just jumped right in and discovered that I had what it took to merge people into the environment. So, that's how I first discovered the skills to be able to do that, because it's not actually something I ever learned. It was just something I did.

After that I was on the downhill from my breakup and as an artist, art is usually where things go when you feel like that. I started to paint everybody into everything.

I was painting people into walls, chairs, backgrounds and all types of things. Then one day I was in Canberra at a festival and I saw the landscape was layered and so beautiful. I just had this vision of how incredible it would be to merge a human into the actual land itself. I distinctly remember thinking, "Wow it's impossible, you couldn't do it", and I let the thought just go.

A few months later I left Australia and I took myself to Peru. I was on a big healing mission and I followed the calling to the medicine in the Amazon. I was divinely led to this one woman who was an 80-year-old Shaman who lived in Iquitos, that's where I sat my first ceremony with Ayahuasca.

In short, it was a week of seeing people painted into the world. There were other things going on, but that was the continuous thread throughout every moment. Seeing people blended into the earth, painting people and painting the Earth itself. So I came out of those ceremonies fully charged with this mission to paint people into the Earth and that's what I did.

I made a little post on a Facebook group saying that I'm doing an art series and I'm opening the space for whoever wants to get painted into the Earth and I was inundated with people that wanted that to happen. I painted around 21 people in a month. I'd basically go on this mysterious adventure with somebody onto a part of the land they resonated with. There was no one else there, just us so it was a very raw process and amazing things happened. Every day this incredible art piece would come to life and I would put it out into the world on Facebook.

**Kim: Wow, that is incredible. Having sat with the medicine in Peru myself, I love that that was the vision Ayahuasca gave you in ceremony. That really hits me in the heart.**

**Is there a commonality with the reasons behind why people come to you to be painted into the world?**

Orly: They want to honor themselves. They want to honor something bigger than their personality and their

identity. To dissolve into the Earth and to tap into something greater than any description of self could ever master.

I think that as time has gone on, the people that come to me are often people who want to celebrate a milestone in life. They either turn a certain age, have been through a trauma or something big in their life, they're pregnant, or they're a couple that have been together for 50 years. Or they're a new couple that are about to get married. There's also been people who have been very sick with cancer and want to leave something behind for their family. It's been amazing.

It's really coming down to landmark moments of life and honoring for self-love. A huge part of it is honoring our physical bodies in all their imperfect majesty and just allowing ourselves to be seen.

One element of my work, is that I keep the rights to all of my pieces. Part of that, is that it's very important for me to be able to show these pieces. Not just as an artist, but also because I truly believe that there's something about being equal with the Earth that resonates in some primitive primal part of our brain. That knows that this is true, that knows a part of the Earth, and that when we see it visually, that there's a resonance that is consciousness awakening.

So, every time I do a piece, people sign off that they will be related for the world to see without a name or without a tag to show.

It's definitely part of the process to be seen and to disappear to be seen.

There's a lot of contrast in the work and they're in this like, epic state of stillness. It can be quite painful and challenging. It's sort of really personal and I'm in a frenetic back and forth state of movement. So, there's this alchemy between stillness and movement as well and that's a very strong dynamic.

**Kim: Just being in that stillness and needing to keep that pose would be therapeutic on some level, like when we step into a space of healing like a workshop or a therapy session.**

**It could potentially have the same kind of impact I would think. I'd be curious what the feedback from your clients is, in how it's changed them throughout the whole painting process?**

Orly: It's been amazing. As I've gone on, I've learnt how to step it up better and better, so that people have some guidance about where to take themselves in those spaces when they're feeling struggles, like connecting to the breath.

But allowing someone to melt into themselves and hear their

Image Credits: Orly Faya's Professional Collection

minds and we talk as well, there's that therapeutic element to that. It's a really intimate space and I'm gravely aware of my responsibility as a fully dressed person in a space with a body who is undressed. There's this vulnerability that's very real. They're not just a canvas, but a human being in my care, which I take really seriously. At the same time, it allows us to have their discomfort because it's definitely a part of growth to be uncomfortable, so I just allow people to go through that space.

The way people talk about it afterwards (and I have got that many testimonials), it was nothing like they thought it was going to be.

**Kim: What other benefits does this process have for people?**

Orly: Body image is a big part of it and I think that only tells a bit of the story. The way we relate to our body vehicles, is really important for our health. For our bodies to work in their best capacity, they also need to be seen, loved and appreciated. Just like we do, just like everything does.

Like with any healing process I do feel that whatever somebody wants to get out of it they can and I'm not able to give them that, they have to receive it. We don't heal each other, we heal ourselves.

So, I create a space in which somebody can step in with as much or as little of their spirit as they would like.

**Kim: Is there a preparation process that your clients go through?**

Orly: Absolutely. From the minute that they book the session and go into our first session together, it is really about starting from where we're at and seeing what is going on in their life. What's the main thing that they want to step into for themselves in their lives? What are they wanting to release and let go of? So when we do come to the day of production, we're really clear about the intentions of why we're doing it and what there is to receive and let go of.

# It's a ceremony, it's a ritual.

So when we come together, we do a ceremony before and we bring through all of those intentions that we've talked about at length. We'll do at least two to three sessions together before we paint because I just feel it's really important to have our energies connecting before that moment, so that everything's very safe and clear.

I work a lot from the studio these days, so the outdoor merges are still available, but they are different products. So, in studio emerging, it's a lot more nurturing and nourishing. It's a controlled environment so we can do any background at all, including any nature scapes, art, abstract backgrounds, colors, movement.

I know people love the idea of being outside and it's very romantic, but the reality of it is, it's tough, challenging and it's not ideal for everyone.

I recently painted my mom into Lake Louise in Alaska which was where she was last with my father on holiday before he died. She really was transported there because that's where her memories were and that's where that last joy of time was with him. Now she has this 1.2-meter artwork above her head of her landscape in that spot which is so precious. What that feels like for her is totally indescribable. So, what's made possible with the studio is that we don't need to actually depend on the sunlight or the rain or the light or the elements of high. People who are pregnant or unwell, get to have breaks. There's no time pressure. It's a much more secure space and way of doing it.

I think that from that, there's a lot more therapeutic essence that can come through actually. Like, I really do feel like it's more therapeutic, healthier and there's studio space.

**Kim: I can really see the benefits from a healing perspective of being safe and held. It would certainly be a consideration for me. What message do you hope to convey to the world by painting people into the Earth?**

Orly: I hope that the artwork does the work of awakening people to the most foundational truth of our lives, which is that we came from the Earth, we are not put here by anyone, we literally fungused out of this planet. Where our spirits come from is a different story, but as a physical body and a being and a creature, we are part of the Earth. We can't live without it and we aren't above or beyond this. We are completely connected. It's our mother. It's our source and there's this beautiful harmony of heaven on Earth that we could be living in.

Right now we're in such crucial time and I would love people to trust nature and also understand that the death is a part of this story.

We're part of everything and I want spirit consciousness to reawaken.

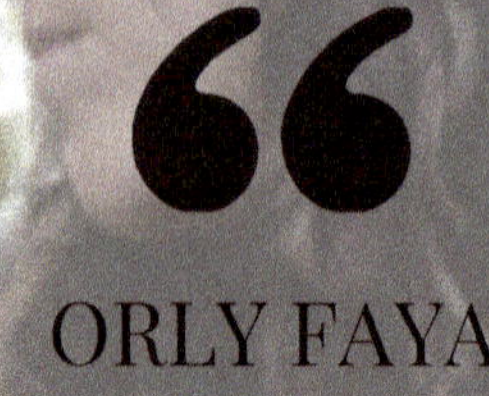

ORLY FAYA

# WHERE OUR SPIRITS COME FROM IS A DIFFERENT STORY, BUT AS A PHYSICAL BODY AND A BEING AND A CREATURE, WE ARE PART OF THE EARTH.

Image Credits: Only Faya's Professional Collection

**Kim: : Now, there's only one of you, not everyone will be able to have their body painted into the Earth by you. What if someone wanted to feel or have that experience of being connected to the Earth through this form of art?**

**How could they perhaps do that for themselves? Or is there something that you would advise them to do to build up that connectedness to Mother Earth?**

Orly: That's a great question. Definitely take time to be in the nature and really connect with the senses. To feel the grass under bare feet. To walk in the rain occasionally. To go in the ocean, when possible. Then to breathe from the belly and smell and notice what's going on; the sound, the smells, the sensations. I think that's what my work really does, it brings people into that. It's a physical process painting somebody and sensation is a big part of it.

When you're in a truly silent place with no sound, it's so different and we have so much sound to notice. So between our breath and our senses, that is a great practice and the results are measurable in our life without a doubt.

**Kim: : Is there anything else that you feel is important for our readers to know about you or your work?**

Orly: I've done this for almost 10 years now. This is my number one passion and it really is such a divine magical journey. I had no grand plan of doing something so niche and bizarre. But because I've now honed this craft so much, I would love more than anything for people to know how valuable this work is and to come and see me while I am still available.

A lot of my clients, they are coming back 6, 7 years later and I can't even believe I'm still painting people. I would love to always be able to offer it, but I just don't know. But now, I'm in my studio in Randwick, NSW and really excited for people to come when they can. I know it's a really crazy difficult time.

**Kim: Last question Orly, what is your Fierce Truth?**

Orly: My fierce truths are that things are not what they seem. The universe is greater than we can imagine.

Life on earth is the greatest miracle.

Non-physical phenomena is foundational. Courage is the key and finally, truth is relative.

responsive
heart
hearing
listening
comm
emotion understanding
emp
presence
relationship awareness
conn
authenticity consciousn
comp
emotional
compa
speak
he
mu

# HEALING GRIEF

With Kim Bleeze

The grief that accompanies the death of someone you love can smash you like a tonne of bricks, and take away your ability to remember how to breathe. And regardless of who you are, it is undoubtedly something that you will most likely experience throughout your life.

It can be a challenging path to navigate, and it is important to remember you are not alone. In this ongoing series, we connect with our readers and discuss their experiences with loss, grief and healing. For this issue, I got to hang out with Radesha (Desh) Dixon, author, coach and speaker. Talking through the death of her auntie who was as close to her as a sister.

**Kim: Radesha, I understand you lost someone very close to you last year. Who was that?**

*Radesha: I lost my aunt but she was more like my sister. We grew up together and we're only four years apart.*

**Kim: Can you talk to me about what happened?**

*Radesha: It was completely unexpected. She wasn't feeling well and called another family member, but she didn't reach them. Then she called daddy and talked to him.*

### That was the last conversation she had.

*I was at a friend's house and didn't see that my mother had called me a few times. I pulled over before I got home to talk to her and she told me that my sister had passed away. I immediately vomited. I had just talked to her the day before and we were discussing what she was going*

to do for the Super Bowl. To go from that to having to bury her, I don't even know how to describe that.

### It leaves you empty and feeling like nothing matters anymore.

*There's a lot of confusion and upset, in the sense that we felt the 911 people didn't get to her in time. She was home but the doors were locked and they were circling the house until at some point, they decided to knock down the door. I guess by the time they got there she was towards the end. We felt like if they had knocked down the door sooner, they would have been able catch it.*

*For me especially I was like, 'Why didn't she call me?'. I could have gotten there sooner. So many things go through your head as to what could I have done differently.*

**Kim: It would have been a very extremely difficult time. How did that personally affect you?**

*Radesha: It knocked me out and I feel empty. My number one supporter was gone and you just don't get over it in a year. I talk to her picture and that's somewhat therapeutic for me.*

*It's unimaginable and you don't ever think something like that will happen to someone close to you, that you talk to and see regularly. It's changed everything including my perspective on life.*

**Kim: In what way did your perspective on life change?**

*Radesha: We hear the cliche, "oh tomorrows not promised, live your best life" and no one really pays attention to that. Then when you get hit with something like this and you're trying to pick up the pieces, it changes everything because that cliche phrase really comes into play. It's like okay, time to do the self-reflection, time to figure out where my life is. Am I happy? What's really going on and what do I need to change?*

**Because if I can talk to you today and I have to bury you tomorrow, that's a whole different ball game. That's a whole different consciousness that I wasn't even remotely ready for, or to have to dive into within myself.**

*So, I definitely look at life differently. I don't do anything I don't want to do anymore. I'm not wasting my time with anything that is really not bringing peace anymore. I needed the positive change and in the midst of all this transformation I think what grows to the surface is probably the path that I should have always been on in the first place.*
*So yeah, my perspective is that I'm not wasting time and I'm pretty much only doing the things that really matter to me.*

**Kim: Thank you for sharing such a vulnerable and heartfelt story. Experiencing grief is really hard. What are some of the strategies or tools that helped you?**

*Radesha: I would say allowing myself time to grieve and that's still ongoing. I also got a chance to be still, and I think a lot of people need to somehow pause in their life. Because if you're busy, you're probably missing some of what your spirit is trying to tell you.*

*In addition, I talked to four bereavement counsellors and then I had my friends. One in particular had lost her mother at the time so she fully understood what I was going through and how I felt. I think the universe brought us together in synchronicity at that time, because we fully understood what it was like.*

*It really made a difference to have someone that understood, I think it aided in my process of grieving.*

**Kim: It's beautiful that you were surrounded by support and people to call on when you needed it. What does your grief look like now? I imagine it's still quite fresh for you.**

*Radesha: It is definitely still fresh, it's a day-by-day process and it's very rough. I just think people have to find strength because we're still alive, that means that we still have purpose and there's something greater. I try to keep that in mind, but it's one foot in front of the other and allowing myself to feel the feelings of what I need to and not try to force myself to be better just because a year has passed.*

*So, I just believe everyone in this position just needs to give themselves grace.*

**Kim: Do you have any advice for our readers that may be struggling themselves?**

*Radesha: I recommend speaking to someone and grief definitely reinforces the importance of self-care on such a high level. You're hurting and what can happen is that you can get depressed, you may not eat, or you eat excessively, or you just don't want to get out of bed. I've been there, it feels like nothing matters.*

*I think part of this is also soul searching and that something is trying to emerge from our soul. The only way that we'll get the clarity of what that is, is if we go through the process and allow ourselves time to grieve. Then whatever feelings come up, let them and deal with them. So I would say do not, in any way, deny what you're feeling. I would also recommend journaling.*

**You can't go through something in atrocity like this and certain things not come up. At some point you can look at that and maybe know what your soul is trying to say.**

You've got
this

Just keep
going

# The *Miracle* of Metatron

## Cultivating a **Relationship** With The Hand of The *Divine*

By John Bride

**Angels are big news.**

Their appeal is attracting. They are celestial helpers who are readily available to rush in and aide us in our hour of need. We are already comfortable asking the likes of the mighty Archangel Michael for his powerful wings of protection and to be soothed and held by the healing hands of Archangel Raphael. These Archangels are as familiar to us as our best friends and family.

But did you know that there is a huge, divine illuminated being who holds vast cosmic power, knowledge and who already knows you better than you know yourself? A being so high, that he can help you move mountains with ease and grace? Let me introduce you to the Archangel Metatron.

The magnificent Archangel Metatron the manager of all known light in our universe and manager of all other Archangels and Masters. Light holds angelic knowledge, codes of healing, spiritual potential and truth. Archangel Metatron is the angel who oversees our personal and collective ascension process. It is a role he holds with deep honour and respect.

Archangel Metatron has been present since the conception of this universe. He witnessed the birthing of the earth and all that we have experienced. He knows both the highs and the lows of our evolution, which makes him the most perfect angelic ally for life's journey. Metatron knows the human personality deeply; he has empathy for us. He understands us fully as humans, and therefore can appreciate the challenges we face. He lends a hand that leads us through the processes of growth.

Archangel Metatron is already present in your life. Your soul knows him. It is simply that your mind that hasn't yet perceived his mentorship. At this critical point in our development, Metatron has stepped

forward to usher us into the new age that awaits.

We are collectively witnessing a profound shift of energy that is taking place on the planet. There has never been such a sacred time to grow and evolve. This is a critical time in our world; fear is reigning supreme.

There is no awareness of duality, no fairness and very little truth. Our physical vison is clouded, but our spiritual sight is awakening. Many people have lost the aspect of love and instead become invested in mania, war, terror, aggression, anger, lies, poverty and hate. Acts of worry and chaos both in the world and ourselves, is present. We are drowning in our own self-indulgence.

Metatron knows that you are trying to rise above the clouds of the intense psychic imprisonment that holds you ransom to your fears and worries. He is here to show you that there is another way, a better way to move forward.

Meta means "beyond a concept" and Tron means "tools." Together Metatron is a sacred tool that takes you beyond the concept of what you are and what you are experiencing now. A hand that leads you and guides you from the bottom upwards towards the light.

Cultivating a relationship with Metatron now is essential. This will enable you to fearlessly move forward with unshakable faith, to find the blessings and the beauty in life once again. He is happy to lead you. You simply have to follow.

Although a majestic being, Archangel Metatron is ready to gift you his friendship and guidance.

# Cultivating a relationship with
## Archangel Metatron

By speaking out loud to the Archangel Metatron, you are making an affirmation. This strengthens your personal belief in the importance and the reality of whatever you are seeking to shift or remedy. Including a message of gratitude is of utmost importance. Gratitude opens the heart chakra, silences the voice of the ego and sends pulses of pure light

to the Archangels. This in turn illuminates your energy field allowing you to receive and plug into Metatron's guidance more freely. Whenever you need a celestial solution, simply tell Metatron. Speak to him as if it was a conversation with an old friend, for Metatron knows the truth of your heart. Be open to receiving intuitive nudges as a response from him. Follow your inner guidance.

Get a journal and devote it solely to increasing communication between you and Archangel Metatron. This is a sacred and personal place where you can write Metatron a letter and ask for assistance in specific ways that are unique to you.

While Metatron knows the truth of your worries and questions, it can be a sacred space to use your free will to ask for help and guidance. You can also use this journal to record any important signs and answers that he sends. Write Metatron a letter at the beginning of the week. Begin the process by expressing thanks about anything in your life that you think he has helped you with recently. Then spend a few sentences free writing, asking him for help or guidance on a specific issue that you need to gain clarity on. For the rest of the week, watch for synchronicities, nudges and signs from your Metatron regarding this issue.

You can also connect to Archangel Metatron in nature. Nature holds a bounty of answers to the deepest of our questions. Get outside, wherever that may be and begin a divine dialogue with him inside of you mind. Pose to him your questions and deepest desires and allow the signs of destiny to reply. Pay attention to the way the wind blows when you speak, watch for the movement of animals and insects, listen to the song of the trees as you pass. These are all confirmations to that, which you seek. Metatron uses the natural forces of nature to inspire, uplift and soothe us.

When you begin to cultivate a relationship with Metatron, you will notice that the world around you begins to change for the better.

You begin to effortlessly transcend the human ego and tap into higher wisdom. Metatron's friendship, mentorship and inspiration, places you in a vibration where you hold the love you are so strongly seeking. Welcome this being into your life, so the miracle of Metatron can manifest.

John Bride is an internationally acclaimed Psychic Medium and voice of Metatron. He is the founder of the Metatron Methods healing training programme that has practitioners globally sharing the light of Metatron's wisdom. He is available for his clients to work with Metatron in psychic readings and healings.

Visit his website at: johnbridepsychic.co.uk

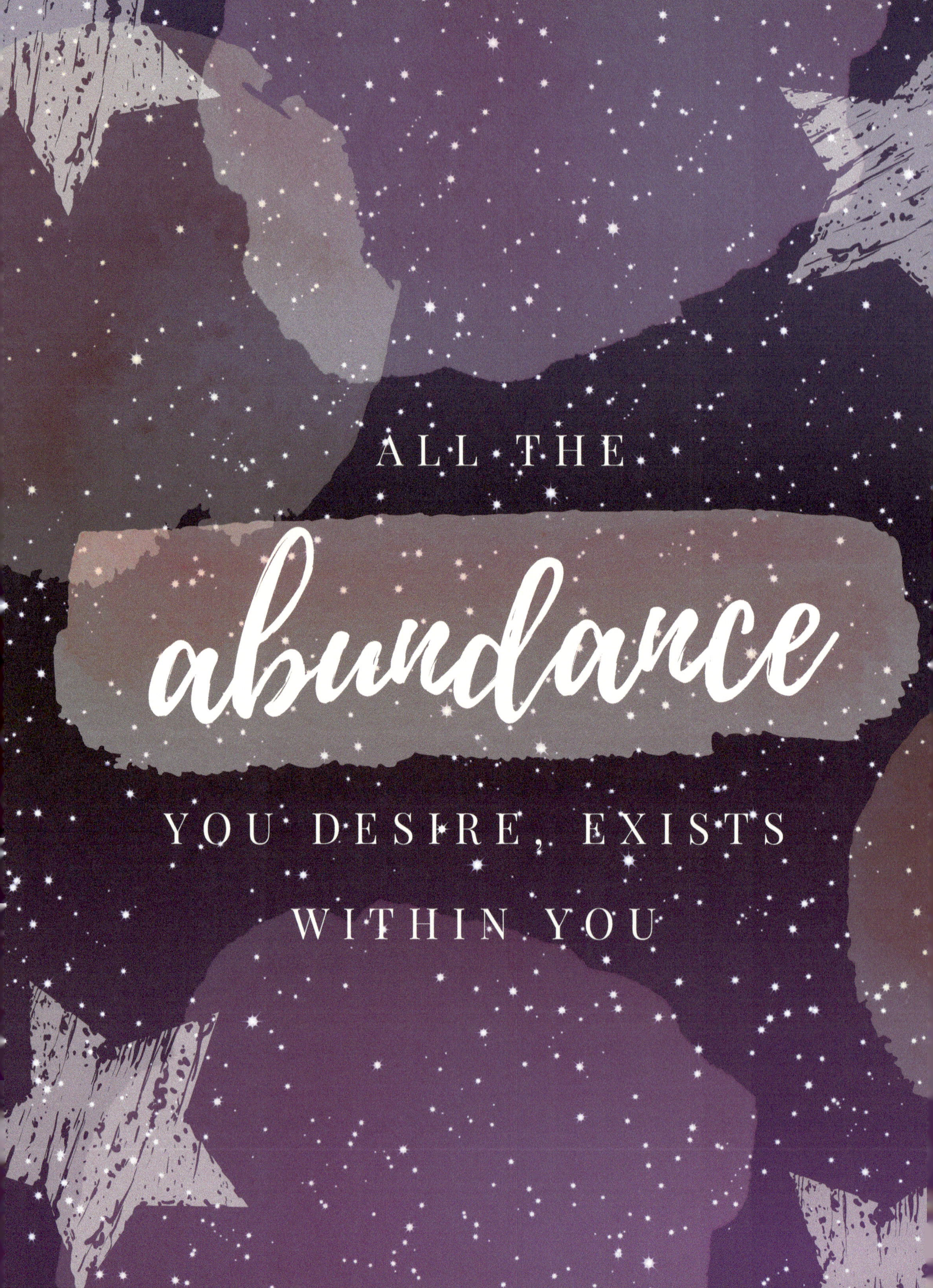

ALL THE
abundance
YOU DESIRE, EXISTS
WITHIN YOU

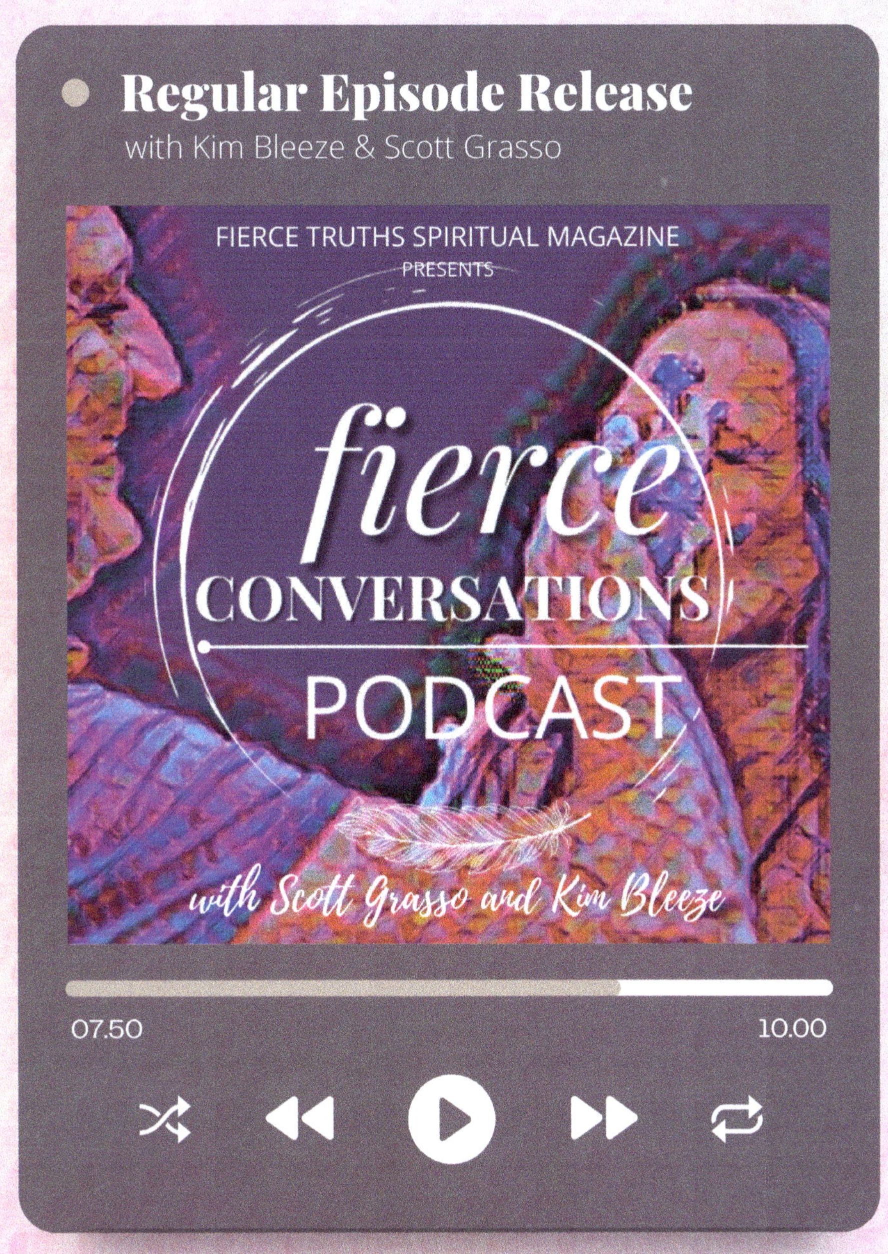


# Fierce Conversations Podcast

## STREAMING NOW

FIERCETRUTHSMAGAZINE.COM/LISTEN-PODCAST

# SELFLESS

By Carrie Myers

## LESS YOURSELF

**I said this to a friend recently. We have been chatting and trying to figure out this Mid-Life thing. Both of us have three kids and a husband. We are searching for where we might have lost ourselves along this path of life. Constantly making sure everyone is taken care of, the house clean, the laundry done, kids at every activity and being cheerleaders for everyone, we forgot to cheer for ourselves. Now that the kids are almost grown, we are struggling, as the identity we thought defined us is walking out the door to make their own lives.**

We are longing for the wild that has been suppressed, folded and put neatly in the closet for that "just in case" time. But now that wild feels moldy, tarnished and out of date.

Have we grown too old to live fully once again? Have our responsibilities squashed our passions? Please know that each of our precious children are beyond anything that we could have ever wished for, hoped for and worked for! There is not one moment we would trade for all that our kids have given us,

taught us and filled our heart with!

It is just "What now? Who am I? Where do I belong? What defines me as a woman? How is my marriage defined, now that our kids do not need us as much anymore? Do we even know our husbands?"

We have selflessly given, not only to our families, but to the schools, charities, neighbors, our homes and careers. Setting aside our needs, wants and desires to meet everyone else where they are/were and never asking

We are longing for the wild that has been suppressed, folded and put neatly in the closet for that "just in case" time.

anyone to meet us where we are. Or maybe asking and being met with resistance. We always seem to be moving towards them, not us.

We traded our romance novels for story books. We traded our manicures for digging in the sand and building sandcastles. We traded our pressed work clothes for yoga pants, ponytails and days at the park. And what amazing days we had at the park! We traded boardrooms and meetings for giggles and sticky hands. What a gift to hold a sweet, little, sticky hand...

Now, we hand them the keys to our cars and pray over them to return home safely, closing the door and shedding a few tears as they drive away. Alone in the house it is quiet, peaceful for just a few minutes. Maybe too quiet. We look at our hands, as the lines have started to form and we notice that they are not as agile as they used to be, nor soft, nor useful. We pour a glass of wine and stare out the window. We wonder, "Now what?"

It starts to seep in that we are not needed as much as we once were, not even to drive them to a friends house to hang out. The heaviness of midlife settles beside us in the chair and reaches its cold, bony fingers toward our wrists. Those fingers want to grab us and bind us, pulling us into nothingness and despair. Oh, but we have made a plan to resist those hands.

We have realized that we have been less ourselves. We become ready to dive into our essences and to revive those silly girls who thought they had life figured out at 23.

Now at 50, we are questioning if life is ever figured out and that we must continue to question everything. We have vowed to share this with our children too. We tell them, "Go, live, be wild, have fun," because there is no reason to grow up so very fast. Of course, we want them to be responsible, but we want to them to breathe in that youth, the curiosity of

it all and to ask those hard questions! We have decided that we are! We are going to live, travel, take pictures and dance naked in the moonlight if that is what stirs us! We will live, laugh, love and leap from tall buildings after we watch the sunset from way up top with our evening cocktail.

"We will not only land on our feet, but we will land in 5-inch stilettos!"
- H. Iden.

Midlife is just another box to check, but it is not a defining downward spiral. We are not Self Less, we are now Self Fulfilling!

Carrie J. Myers writes mostly poetry reflecting life phases and the processes of her journey along the way. Through yoga practices, she found words that held higher meaning and growth. She hopes to inspire change in the souls of her readers so they discover their authentic selves and revive, create their light within.

Visit her at carriemyersauthor.com

# FIERCE TRUTHS MAGAZINE

## Read us all the ways!

## ...now available in print!

THE MORE

*grateful I am*

THE MORE

BEAUTY I SEE

- Mary Davis

# EASY GUIDE TO

## Giving Water Readings

Written by Kim Bleeze
Fierce Truths Magazine

While not entirely common, Water Readings can be an accurate and fun way to receive psychic and intuitive information about your sitter.

Almost everything holds an energetic imprint, and we also leave energy residue on everything we touch, which means, everything we touch can potentially be used to 'read' us. As long as it is clean of other people's energy of course.

**In fact, this technique has been used in the past by healers in some Indigenous cultures by getting their patients to place their hands in a bowl of water. The healer would then place their hands in the water after and intuitively 'read' them.**

If nothing else, it would certainly be something fun to try!

## Step 1

Find a quiet and comfortable place to set up your equipment.  Fill your large bowl with distilled water without placing your own hands inside as yes. Give it a swirl and leave it to settle for 5-10 minutes.

## Step 2

Ask your sitter to sit facing the bowl, getting them to place their hands in the water and gently move them around for 1-2 minutes. They can remove their hands and give them a dry when time is up.

## Step 3

1.Close your eyes, take a deep breath, relax and submerge your own hands in the same water, moving them around gently and slowly. Pay attention to every detail. Rule of thumb is, that whatever comes up for you throughout a reading, is always relevant to your sitter.

## Step 4

What information are you receiving? Focus on the images, thoughts, feelings and knowingness that begins to drop into your awareness through your mind, and the feelings in your hands.

## Step 5

Tell your sitter everything you receive!

There are many great techniques you can use to receive psychic information and Water Reading is a great tool to try regardless of what level of development you are at.

It adds a splash (pun intended) of fun and versatility to your practice and aids you to receive information in a new and exciting way.

INSTANT ACCESS

MINI COURSE START TODAY

Tap into Your Potential

AND EMBRACE WHAT YOU WHERE BORN TO DO

Redefine Your Passion
Discover Your Purpose
Clarify Your Pathway

fiercetruthsmagazine.com/explore-yourself

# monthly musings

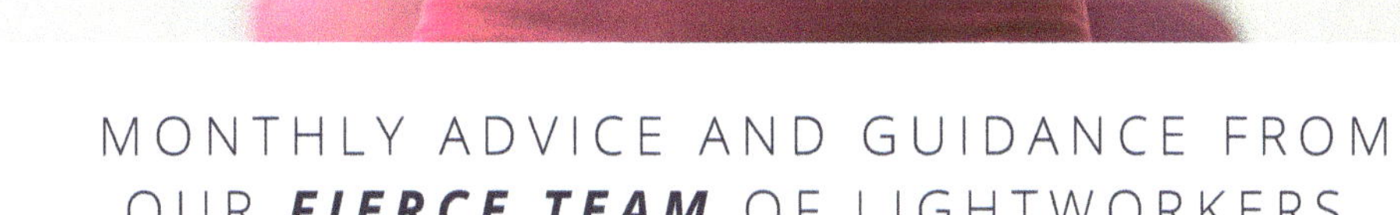

OUR *Fierce* **Experts**

MONTHLY ADVICE AND GUIDANCE FROM
OUR **FIERCE TEAM** OF LIGHTWORKERS

## LINDIE GUNSTON
### *Spirit and Soul*

...is a South African born psychic, medium, and teacher based in Geelong, Vic, who is passionate about teaching psychic and mediumship development and serving Spirit.

## SCOTT GRASSO
### *Radical Thinking*

...is an intuitive, psychic, medium, mentor and apart of our editing team. He has a passion to guide people out of the fear and darkness so they can live a joyful life.

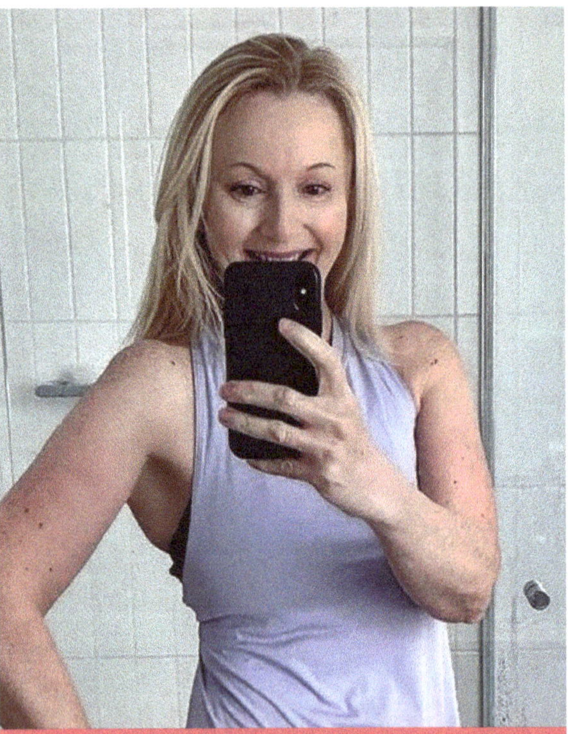

## JO LASTRO
### *Fierce Fitness*

...is a 1st degree Muay Thai kickboxer and fitness coach. She loves to feel comfortable in her own skin and inspires others to overcome their own obstacles and feel the same.

## KARINA BARCA
### *Empowered Healing*

...is a medium, healer, psychic, reiki master, teacher, mentor and forensic healing practitioner. Her passion is to serve, inspire and assist all who want to grow, heal and evolve.

## LISA WESTGATE

### *Mind Your Mental Wellness*

...is an Award Winning Mental Health Advocate, speaker, trainer, best-selling author. Also creator of The Misfit Hub, a support for weirdos, freaks and unicorns to live a life of zero f*cks.

## ELOISE FIELKE

### *Plant Wisdom*

...is and Intuitive, Psychic Medium, development teacher, Kinesiologist, Mind-Body Medicine Practitioner and developing Shamanic Ceremonialist/Spirit Weaver.

## MICHELLE LUEHMAN

### *SpiritWise*

Michelle is a healer, guide, spiritual coach and philosopher. She combines her innate spiritual work with what she has learnt through her spiritual studies and business skills.

## FIERCE EXPERT

### *Your Own Regular Column*

Are you our next Fierce Expert?
Visit our website to learn how you can become apart of our family. Perhaps now is the time to start sharing your souls message with the world.

# MIND Your Mental Wellness

By Lisa Westgate

According to the pastel-coloured memes on social media, self-care is apparently taking a bath or getting a massage. I like a day at the spa as much as anybody, but that's a day. You see true self-care is more than one day of pampering.

It's things like boundaries, saying 'no' and radical self-ownership. It's about putting yourself higher up on your priority list, being decisive about who gets your time and energy.

You may be in a similar position to where I was seven years ago, sitting on my couch wondering "What the f*ck am I going to do with my life?" At that point, self-love was aspirational. Then there is the other end of the spectrum and that's self-loathing.

I could have run a course on self-loathing. I had years of practise and I was fantastic at it. I knew all the thoughts to think and all the ways of speaking to myself with disgusting and abusive language. Things I would never say out loud to another person.

If that's the way you are feeling, I want to reassure you that there is an opposite to self-loathing. If you have had capacity for self-loathing, then you must also have within you somewhere the capacity for self love.

How do you get from the low end of the emotional spectrum to the higher end? The answer is that you do it in steps.

If you're at the point where you're really speaking negatively to yourself, the next step up is to self-like. Work on accepting who you are right now. Accept that all of you, flawed or otherwise, is you.

There's always room for improvement of course, but the journey of growth is to identify those areas and then make shifts in that direction. If you met you, out at the shops, would you like yourself? Probably. For instance, if you're a good person; you 'd hold the door open for people, right? As long as you keep taking steps forward, you're moving in the right direction.

We know self-love exists because the opposite exists. We spent enough time in that opposite end. So, if self-love and fierce self-love is something that fees far out of the realm of possibility for you right now, just take one step at a time. Break things down into small pieces that are achievable. You don't have to achieve self-love in a randomly assigned period of time.

Let's do a quick thought experiment. Imagine that you are the boss of your time and your energy. You have dumped all the crap that doesn't serve you anymore. You have developed some new beliefs by writing down some rules around how you feel about yourself, how you talk to others, what you value in the world and what you believe.

Imagine you were able to love yourself fiercely for who you had grown into and who you had become. You respect yourself and treat yourself like your own best friend, instead of your own personal bully. How does life look? What do you want that to look like? What if that was your life in six months? What if that was life in three months? What would that mean to you?

I often have clients who say "Two weeks ago was a really good week, but then last week I didn't have such a great week." They tell me why they feel they moved backwards. I remind them that it is all part of the dance and that the dance is backwards steps and forward steps. Every step will get you further along to where you're going, but it's not a straight line forward.

Keep in mind, key elements of self-love are self-compassion and self-forgiveness. You can't bully yourself into self-love. This is not an end-outcome focus. It's a transformational journey, step by step. One that I guide and support my clients through.

One thing we look at together is 'the power of proximity.' You are the sum of the five closest people around you. How do the people around you speak to you? How do they speak to themselves? It's important to be mindful and deliberate about the input you are allowing to enter your mind. Having people around you that set a good example can be a real advantage.

Another tip is to consume supportive media in the form of books, podcasts and courses. Find ways to educate yourself on your journey to self-love, through the life lessons of others. It can help to know that you are not alone on the path. Find a supportive tribe online and offline, to help keep you forward focused.

### Work towards developing an unshakeable belief in yourself.

This comes as you rediscover or redefine who you really are and learn to embrace who you are. Treat yourself with the unconditional love and compassion you would a small child, because you were one and are still deserving of that love.

Be curious and kind and watch what happens. Happy Releasing.

Much Love Lisa. xx

# RADICAL THINKING

*By Scott Grasso*

## PRACTICING FORGIVENESS

> 66
>
> *For you to begin embracing forgiveness, start by forgiving yourself.*

Last month I talked about the harmful nature of resentments, how toxic they can be, and how to release them. Let's look now at expanding our spiritual devotions to include the noble virtue of forgiveness.

### What exactly is forgiveness?

According to Wikipedia: "Forgiveness is the intentional and voluntary process by which one undergoes a change in feelings and attitude regarding a given offense, and overcomes negative emotions such as resentment and vengeance." I am interested in the two words "intentional" and "voluntary." It implies that that I need to work at changing how I view and judge people and situations.

Practicing forgiveness had to begin with how I see myself. Through doing lots of self-work, I understand now that I am far from perfect. Like you, I have big fears and character flaws that frequently interfere with my relationships.

For instance, most of us are afflicted with two types of fear:

**1. That we're going to lose what we have**

**2. That we're not going to get what we want**

When one or both of these fears are active, it triggers a bunch of ugly behaviours. They are often referred to as The Seven Deadly Sins: Pride, Anger, Sloth, Lust, Greed, Envy and Jealousy. And when they are present, I start to gather evidence that people are stupid, bad and wrong. My ego shifts the focus away from my self, so that I don't have to confront or sit with my own unpleasant feelings.

For you to begin embracing forgiveness, start by forgiving yourself for sometimes being a ratbag. For instance, I am a recovering gossip. I delighted in practicing character assassination in order to make my fragile self feel better. The truth is that we are all the precious children of a loving Great Spirit. I have a relationship with a Goddess who loves me unconditionally and wants me to be happy.

If you really want to bust your ego, start practicing forgiveness by inserting the words "like me" in every criticism of others. For instance, "Like me, people can often be inconsiderate and selfish." My 12-Step recovery friends often say, "Like me, people are often wrong and frequently sick." Yuck. It kinda takes the fun out of proclaiming your own righteousness, doesn't it?

Each day, I try to accept that I am just another imperfect bozo on the Life Bus, just like you. My spiritual advisor, a lovely man who I've been working with for 24 years, often says to me: "Scott, when you are perfect, then you can judge others."

## So if I'm not perfect, why do I expect others to be?

Let's talk about some of the benefits of forgiveness. First of all, it burns a lot less energy than holding on to anger. It also sets me free from psychic, energetic and karmic entanglements. When I move out of staying stuck, there's room and perspective for me to

stop wanting to be right, and instead choosing to be happy.

If you relate to all this, I suggest introducing some healing prayers into your daily devotions. Praying for those we resent or hate is difficult, but amazingly transformative. If someone is pissing you off or has hurt you, pray for them for two weeks. Start with the Prayer of Acceptance: "Goddess, save me from being angry. Like me, people are often fearful and frequently sick." Then wish for them every gift and happiness that you want for yourself. You will be totally amazed if you do this, as anger dissipates.

Then recite The Serenity Prayer: "Goddess/Great Spirit, grant me the serenity to accept the things I cannot change; the willingness to change the things that I can, and the wisdom to know the difference."

The third affirmation is a real "clanga," as my Aussie friends say: "I acknowledge, accept and celebrate that I am exactly where I need to be in this glorious moment of Now, in all of my glorious imperfection. And I acknowledge, accept and celebrate that you are exactly where you need to be in this glorious moment of Now, in all of your glorious imperfection." This gives us perspective and the first flowering of compassion, both for our selves and others.

> 66
>
> *When you find yourself feeling hurt or triggered, ask yourself:*
> *"What would Buddha do?"*

Would Buddha complain, gossip or feel victimised? Or would he calmly accept his lot, practicing forgiveness and sending compassionate love to himself and others?

Of course, feel your feelings when someone steps on your toes. Sit with it. Talk to a trusted advisor or guide. But don't stay stuck, judging and criticising. Accept your flawed humanity and the humanity of the other, and send love to everyone. Pray for the highest good and greatest joy for all involved. Then move on with your life, choosing joy.

Namaste, Family.

By Karina Barca

# EMPOWERED HEALING

## SIGNS AND STRATEGIES TO OVERCOME LOW SELF ESTEEM

**This is a topic that a large majority of people and nearly all of my clients, have experienced and had to deal with at some point in their lives.**

Low self-esteem is when you do not think much of yourself, or do not hold yourself in high regard. Having low self-esteem can affect virtually every aspect of your life, such as your relationships, job, health, your future, reaching your goals and reaching your potential.

Poor self-esteem can also affect your thoughts, emotions and behavioural patterns, taking a toll on your emotional wellbeing. It causes you to focus on your flaws rather than your strengths. You tend to blame yourself when things go wrong. This leads you to always finding fault with some aspect of yourself, whether it is your appearance, personality or your capabilities.

## The following are some common signs of low self-esteem:

! Negative self-talk

! Poor confidence

! Lack of control over your life and what happens to you

! Poor outlook on life and the future

! Feeling hopeless

! Worry and self-doubt

! Problems asking for what you need

! Trouble accepting positive feedback

! Lack of boundaries and not reinforcing boundaries

! Fear of failure

! People-pleasing in order to gain external validation

Some other signs are feeling anxious, unlovable, incompetent and having a low body image. You may be worried about judgement and judge yourself too harshly. You may think you are stupid, awkward, different, or worthless. These are all negative beliefs that are really opinions rather than fact.

So with all this in mind, you can see how it plays a powerful role in many areas in your life. This is why having low self-esteem can be such a serious problem and can have such a serious negative impact on your life and wellbeing.

Having awareness around these negative impacts highlights the importance of addressing, healing, and changing the traumas, conditioning, and patterns that have created these negative belief systems.

These belief systems are almost always created in childhood, which can be anywhere between birth and 20 years of age. It could be as simple as a learnt behaviour. For example, growing up with a mother who had low self-esteem, and learning that behaviour from her negative self-talk. It could also stem from something more traumatic such as verbal, physical or sexual abuse. Perhaps you were told that you were stupid or you were criticized and made to feel that you or what you do is never good enough. Maybe you felt invisible or experienced abuse. All of these can have a tremendous effect on you and how you develop your sense of self and your identity.

In Forensic Healing sessions, I dig below the issue itself. I work like an investigator to identify the age at which low self-esteem was anchored into a person. I collect information such as an archetype, negative belief patterns or negative emotions. This can lead to a positive vision of how a client really wants to feel. Then together with the client, we are able to address what was happening at that point in time, how all of the information we have gathered ties into their experience and how it has affected different aspects of themselves and their lives.

When you gain awareness, perspective and understanding as to why you have low self-esteem, you can then begin to rebuild it. We revisit a specific age, acknowledge your inner child and validate your feelings. When this happens, you allow yourself to release it all. Then a great healing can take place. You finally know the exact reason why things have occurred and you release the power of that anchor point. This is how true healing begins.

The next phase of the journey is to rebuild your self-esteem. With the insight you gain during your healing session, you can change behaviours and rebuild your self-esteem by noticing your thoughts, forgiving yourself and practicing self-acceptance. It takes time to change and create new behaviours and patterns for yourself, so be patient.

The beautiful thing is that you will learn to not only like yourself, but also believe in yourself, and believe that you deserve love from yourself and others. You will learn to stand in your power and value yourself, your thoughts, feelings, opinions and interests.

Building self-esteem can also affect your motivation to go after the things you want in life and to achieve short term and long-term goals. It has a positive impact on your relationship with yourself and how you treat yourself. This also affects how you allow others to treat you. This will help with your ability to develop healthy and supportive relationships.

Developing a healthy self-esteem will impact every aspect of you and your life. As it grows, you will feel more positive about yourself. Your confidence, your sense of wellbeing, and your outlook on life will improve. It makes you much more resilient, able to cope with life's ups and downs and also creates more flow in your life.

Get real and raw. Gain awareness and knowledge. Choose to heal, grow, learn and transform. Step into Your Power. Become the Creator of Your Life. This is what I call "Empowered Healing."

Blessings,
Karina xx

# SPIRIT & SOUL

*By Lindie Gunston*

Many developing psychics and mediums have spent years denying who they are, mostly because they've had difficult life experiences. Perhaps these people have needed to work through several layers of healing, before they could build the life experience that is essential to understanding themselves and their souls purpose.

At this point, they are then able to integrate their healing, while also having the insight necessary to experience their soul on a whole new level.

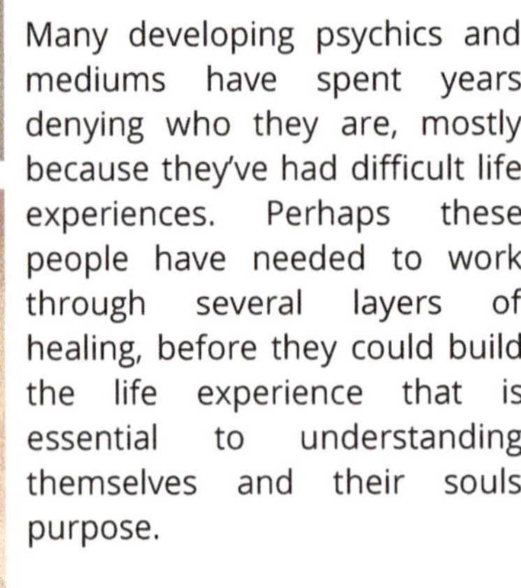

This is a level of understanding where it is no longer possible to deny who they truly are. When they start to understand that the human experience is the driving force that accelerates and elevates their souls growth in the direction of service to Spirit and humanity, the developing medium begins to step into their souls purpose.

The perceived limitation of the physical human experience can often block potential mediums from fully experiencing their souls truth as they, like many souls living through this physical experience, are prone to limiting themselves with the human mind.

One of the biggest blocks in both psychic and mediumship development occurs when people compare themselves to others. They may use other mediums as a measuring stick of where they think they should be in their development, perhaps not taking into consideration that comparison is futile.

We are all a unique and divine expression of the universe and Spirit. When comparison is at play, a developing medium may end up denying their souls truth of who they truly are. They may also forget that they are on Earth to bust through

the limitations of the human experience by stepping into the wisdom of their soul. Such wisdom may have been accumulated over many lifetimes.

Deep down, our soul always knows the truth and that truth whispers to us on a daily basis. Our mind likes to silence this truth by casting doubt on it. How do we listen to our soul? How do we feel into who we really are? Consider ALL of the spiritual experiences you have had — from the day you were born until this very moment. Pretty magical, hey? How might you be blocking your own souls truth by constantly questioning everything, instead of stepping back and ALLOWING your souls truth to be divinely expressed through your human experience?

# THAT'S THE "GRAND" SECRET.
## *YOU JUST NEED TO BE YOU!*

I have spent well over a decade soul-searching and trying to piece together the fragments of my human experience, in order to understand the truth of who I really am. Once I fully grasped the enormity that I am a soul, experiencing what it is like to be human, my world changed forever. I can no longer go back to my old ways. Sure, I still have very "human" moments of anger, frustration and despair, but I consciously take myself back to my souls purpose. I remind myself that I am here to guide, uplift and inspire humanity through my own unique divine expression of my souls purpose.

Recognizing your souls truth isn't easy — it's a constant battle between head and heart. Spirit works so hard to get through to us and many of us will, at some point, recognize our souls calling. That calling is to be of service to humanity and Spirit and to step into your souls purpose. This has always been part of the plan! Our human mind simply needs time to catch up with our souls journey at times.

In the words of Pierre Teilhard de Chardin, "We are not human beings having a spiritual experience. We are spiritual beings having a human experience."

It's time to remember what you came here for: to step into your souls purpose. To be a beacon of light for humanity and Spirit. To own who you truly are!

# FIERCE Fitness

*By Jo Lastro*

## SELF-DISCIPLINE AND EXERCISE:

There are lots of successful people in the world who have achieved their goals and I believe many of you have also achieved your goals, but don't give yourself credit for, or even think about them.

If this is not you, then you may have a friend who has just been promoted at work, or a gym buddy who is in great shape after all the hard work they have put in.

You see what is often less visible, is the hard work behind their success.

Staying true to your healthy eating plan, taking the right supplements for your body and working out, takes a considerable amount of effort and ability called self-discipline. That is the key to success for many. If you master this, then any time you start, is a turning point to get your goals right and become self-disciplined.

Personally, self-discipline is not something you wake up with, it takes hard work.

Self-discipline is like any skill. It needs to be practised. Whilst some people might be naturally good at self-discipline, the majority have to work at it before they become good at it.

### What is self-discipline?

- It is the ability to control our behaviour so that we can avoid temptation and achieve our set goals.

- It is the ability to postpone and withstand undesirable effects.

- It is a limited source of motivation that can be depleted.

- It is being able to resist temptations and focus on what is important.

- It is being able to exert control over one's behaviour, and to do this consistently and reliably over time.

### Is this you?

Are you trying to build self-discipline in your own life in the areas of healthy eating, exercise, meditation or maybe writing or practicing playing the guitar?

You need to remember that you might be doing this for physical health reasons, or you want to try and learn something new that brings pleasure in your life.

I believe you can learn self-discipline and it requires training daily. You will benefit in many ways and it will help you take a more rational approach to things, rather than an emotional one. It will ultimately give you back your power to overcome resistance and accomplish your goals.

> "We all have dreams but to make dreams come into reality, it takes an awful amount of determination, dedication, effort, and self-discipline"
>
> **- Jesse Owens**
> **American athlete and four-time Olympian winner.**

## Exercise:

Many of us think self-discipline is always being at the gym/studio or doing some sort of marathon. Really, it can be also the opposite. Let's look at this a bit closer.

### Starting The Day

*Starting the day with a cold shower is something that requires a lot of self-discipline. It is a simple behaviour that you can easily incorporate into your daily routine.*

*It may not sound ideal, especially on a cold winter's day, but it does wonders for your body.*

### Meditation

*This is a very powerful tool that can help you improve your mental, physical and emotional health. I get it, sitting still for a while, keeping your mind still and preventing it from wandering requires self-control.*

*Honestly, meditation can be a great exercise for anyone who wants to increase their self-discipline.*

### Sleep

*When you get enough sleep, it improves your focus, your mood and your overall health. Did you know that indirectly, sleep assists you when you are trying to increase your self-discipline?*

### Exercise

*My favourite one. Exercising on a regular basis is a great way to improve your self-discipline. It will teach you how to focus on a task at hand and by doing so you learn to preserve and accomplish your goals.*

Self-discipline is so important in exercise, as it is required to achieve optimal health. It is also needed when breaking a habit like smoking or rebalancing after health issues. Those who exercise regularly demonstrate higher levels of self-esteem and maintain a sense of self-discipline.

From my own personal experiences, I know that being self-disciplined at times won't make you popular with your friends. Why? For example, some of my friends don't understand why I have done a number of challenges or why I constantly train and push myself. But that is ok too. You need to remember you are your own competition and your goals are unique only to you.

## Challenges with self-discipline:

As a coach, I see many people come up against challenges with self-discipline daily.

Let me give you an example: One of my clients was suffering from health-related issues, overweight and desperate to get back into shape. Whilst he had signed up to go to a gym, he was having trouble following through. You see, the lack of discipline with exercise was spilling into all areas of his life and he was feeling depleted.

## Some easy-to-remember strategies to build & maintain self-discipline:

- ✓ **Get motivated** – the reason and underlying drive behind why you are doing something.

- ✓ **Remove temptation** – if you want to feel better and eat better, put the junk food away.

- ✓ **Create a goal** – define your specific goal or vision, give yourself a deadline and get moving.

- ✓ **Start small** – change is hard, but if you start slow, you can build momentum without getting overwhelmed.

- ✓ **Be kind to yourself** – you are going to have setbacks along the way, but don't give up. Celebrate your wins, no matter how small they are.

Ask yourself this question. Where would a little more self-discipline have the greatest impact in your life?

## Reward of self-discipline:

Small steps can lead to big victories. It is important to take the first step. Once you do, an amazing journey full of physical and mental self-discovery awaits you. You have the power to become more disciplined. You've got this.

## Something to think about:

I strongly believe in self-discipline and that being good at anything requires focus and practice. Focus on the things that are important to you and do them reliably, in the face of inevitable barriers.

However, I also acknowledge that at times, self-discipline can be difficult to maintain and you may experience failures along the way. But the thing is to acknowledge these failures and/or difficult times and keep on going because one day you will be proud of yourself for not giving up.

# SpiritWise

## Pathways to Spiritual Awakening

*By Michelle Luehman*

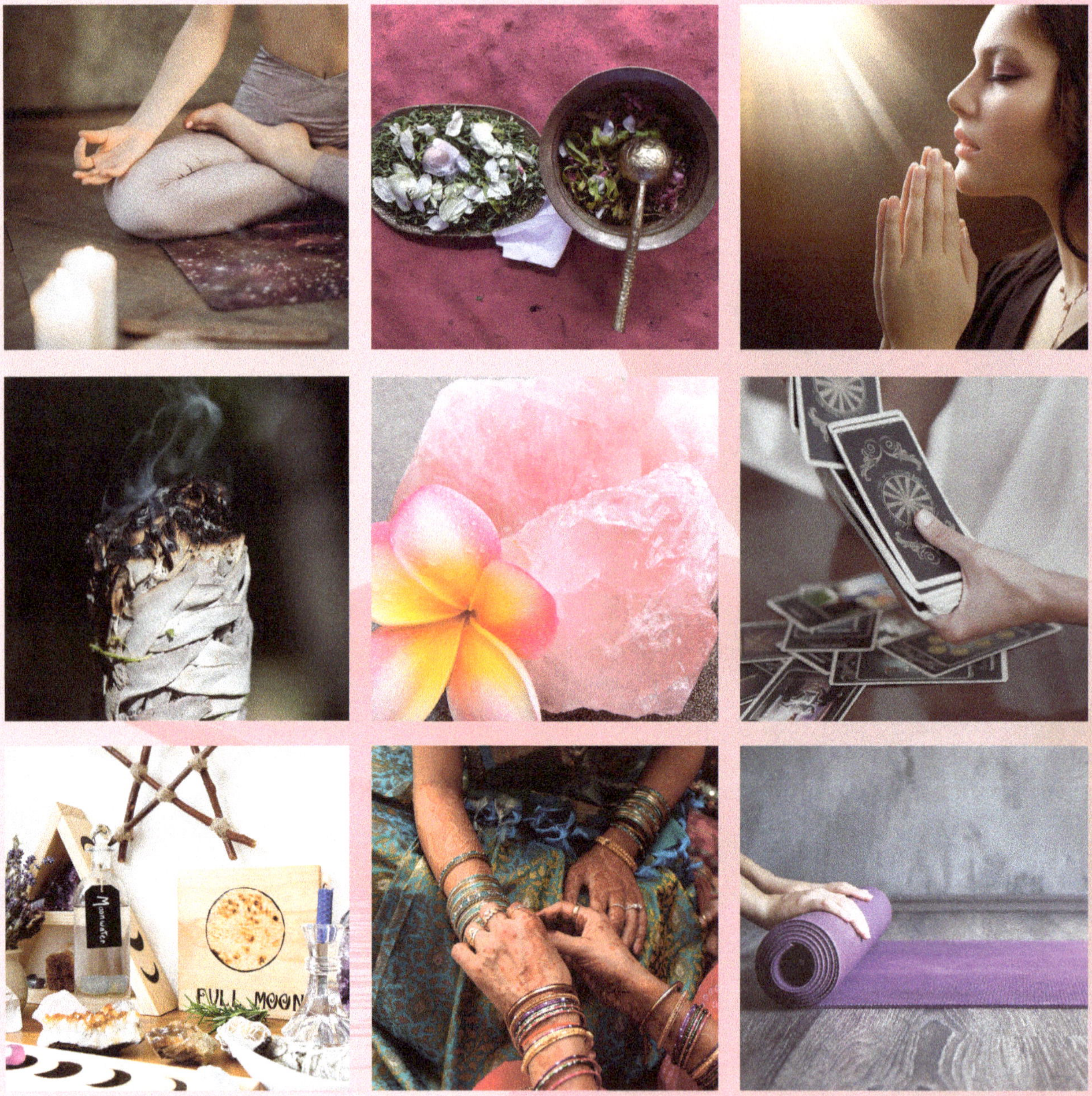

# Signs You Are Spiritually Awakening

Spiritual Awakening comes in all forms and experiences. It means having a sense or awareness of the feelings of connectedness to a universal network of energy. This experience is sensory.

Our intellectual understanding comes afterwards from study, reflection and the transference of information. This is often referred to as downloading. When we are connected spiritually and receiving information through the spiritual super highway, it changes how we see the world.

Our Awakened Spiritual Journey begins when we acknowledge within ourselves that there is more to life than what we logically understand. Our experiences show us glimpses into another landscape.

Our response to these experiences can vary dramatically, but a larger number of us are embracing the ancient wisdoms of Spirituality. You may ask: "What are the physical sensations or signs that we are Awakening Spirituality?" Let's start with the very common experience of overt occurrence of co-incidence. For instance, every time you look at the clock you see double or repeating digits. You increasingly see feathers, stones, objects, birds or animals at unexpected times and places. You are thinking of something or someone and they, or it, appears physically or in a message. You wander into a random shop and find just the thing you were looking for. Once might be coincidence, but repetition is a message.

One day, floating in a pool, I saw continuous cloud formations of phoenix. When I went home, I found a very important message waiting for me.

Likewise, you might hear, see or feel entities. These may be experienced as changes in atmospheric pressure, catching movement out of the corner of your eye, or seeing and hearing people/beings. You might have the feeling that people or beings are with you. These interactions can be a little more unnerving to the uninitiated and they can trigger fear. In me and I hope in you too, they spark a curiosity to continue and learn more.

Theses interactions are a little more earthbound in nature and we are working with spirits rather than working with energies. In my house, I often find things are moved. For instance, the tea tin is found in the pan cupboard. Keys are removed from my bag and found with the towels. This activity did lead to quite a few discussions about boundaries and appropriate behavior, plus some additional space cleansing!

Regardless of how you may respond to these interactions, I recommend that at this stage you take actions to make sure that you and your environment is clean.

A good cleansing ritual is a foundation awakening skill we all must master. Use white sage, clear quartz, selenite crystals, salt, singing bowls, tea tree or eucalyptus oil in a burner. They are all excellent energetic cleaners and easy to use. Cleansing activities will eliminate any negative energy or entities that are not there for your Highest Good. If you feel uncomfortable, you can spiritually & energetically clean your house and space because not everyone has your back on the spiritual super highway.

At night when we are relaxed or even sleeping, is a common time for us to become aware of spiritual activity. We are relaxed, not on guard or preoccupied and therefore more aware of and open to contact. This is when we have high sensory dreams, experience being touched, hear voices and become aware of company or experience intimacy, flight, lightness and levitation.

In my early days, I would often call in both of my Grandmothers to protect me. They were both passed and both formidably protective. Whichever friend or relative that you think will safeguard you, ask them to do so. Likewise, they will bring in whoever they know to help keep you safe. Please remember to ask permission and give thanks to whoever you call in.

Once the spirit world has your attention, is your curiosity peaked enough that you want to go the next step? If you are, what awaits you is a journey like no other. An awakening of your senses to dimensions of heightened awareness, subliminal connection, conscious awakening and Universal Consciousness.

The path you embark on will be one of personal growth, a shedding of several old, even comfortable skins. It's the re-wiring of your mind to embracing new patterns of thought and action. As with all learning, it will take commitment. There may be moments of frustration and even grief as we leave behind what we have known and what has in the past, supported and served us well.

If you can embrace the spiritual path and venture on your unique soul's journey, what awaits is a life of awakenings. A life of emotional and psychological well being that is internally referenced, but existing within a context of being freely externally supported, via a purely harmonious energetic network. You will have moments of pure Nirvana and a relationship with the world which has completely changed how you are and who you are.

**Is that not worth the commitment to**
**YOUR Spiritual Awakening?**

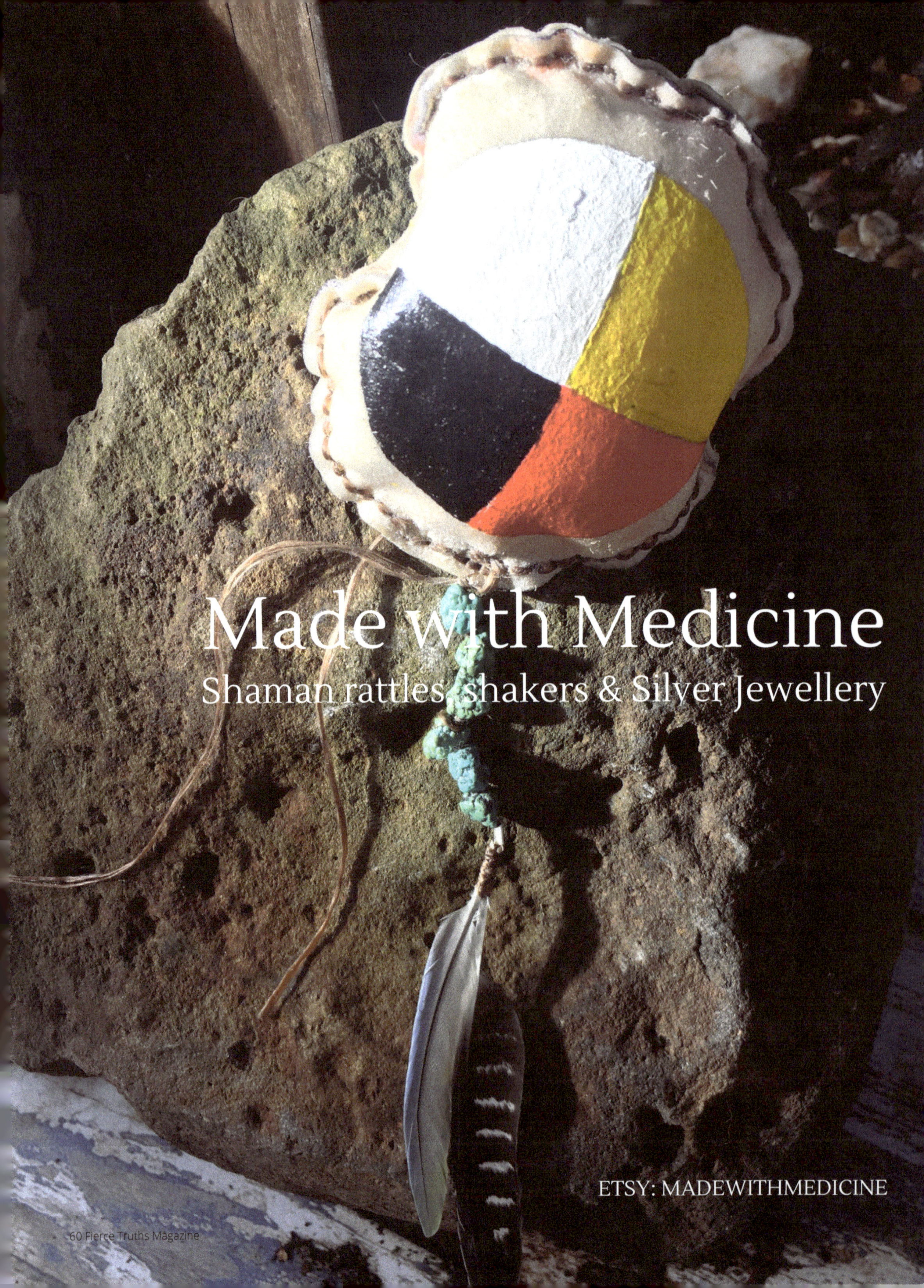
Made with Medicine
Shaman rattles, shakers & Silver Jewellery
ETSY: MADEWITHMEDICINE

www.ingramcontent.com/pod-product-compliance
Lightning Source LLC
Chambersburg PA
CBHW040908070726
47599CB00038B/2347